Car
Games

Car
Games

100 Games to Avoid
"Are we there Yet?"

Jo Pink

PRC

Produced in 2004 by
PRC Publishing Limited
The Chrysalis Building
Bramley Road, London W10 6SP

An imprint of Chrysalis Books Group

This edition published in 2004
Distributed in the U.S. and Canada by:
Sterling Publishing Co., Inc.
387 Park Avenue South
New York, NY 10016

© 2004 PRC Publishing Limited

ISBN 1 85648 727 X

Printed and bound in China

Jacket Acknowledgments:

Classic American Automobiles: front cover center.

CORBIS/Macduff Everton front cover background:
CORBIS/Paul A. Souders front cover bottom center: CORBIS/Chris Collins front cover center right.

Digital Vision: front cover top and back cover.

Picture Credits:

Classic American Automobiles: 14, 22, 25.

Chrysalis Image Library: 82.

CORBIS: © Joseph Sohm; ChromoSohm
Inc./CORBIS, 12; © Morton Beebe/CORBIS, 16;
© GRAHAM TIM/CORBIS SYGMA, 18; © Alan
Schein Photography/CORBIS, 19; ©
Reuters/CORBIS, 40; © Bettmann/CORBIS: 42
© Hulton-Deutsch Collection/CORBIS: 48, © Jeff
Zaruba/CORBIS: 62, © RAULT JEAN
FRANCOIS/CORBIS KIPA, 65.

Digital Stock: 28 (bottom right).

Digital Vision: 10, 20 (bottom center) 20, (center
left), 20 (center right), 20 (top), 27, 28 (bottom
left), 30 (center right), 31, 32, 33, 34, 37, 41,
45 (top center) 45 (center), 46 (top right), 46
(center right), 46 (back right), 47, 49, 50, 56,
57, 60, 61, 70 (bottom right), 71 (bottom), 71
(center right), 72, 73, 78 (top), 78 (bottom right),
78 (bottom left), 85, 86, 87, 91, 92, 93.

Getty Images Royalty Free: 53 (bottom right).

Image100: 61.

PhotoAlto: 71 (top left).

Photodisc: 2, 35, 39, 43, 45 (bottom left),
45(top left), 45 (top right), 45 (bottom right), 54,
55, 58, 63, 79 (top right), 79 (center right), 81.

Rex Features: 74.

Simon Clay (© PRC Publishing) 11, 13, 15, 17,
23 (bottom right), 24 (bottom right), 26, 29.

Stockbyte: 21 (center left), 21 (center right), 30
(bottom left), 36, 45 (bottom center), 59.

Trains of the World: 68, 83 (bottom), 89.

Weatherstock: 38.

Contents

Introduction

Nobody likes a lengthy car journey. Given the choice everyone would sooner get there earlier than later. But until *Star Trek*-type teleporters (or whatever they're called) are actually brought into service we're all stuck with plowing tediously up and down the ever more congested highways of the country to get wherever we're going.

Children, as I've found out over the last twelve years, like to let you know when they're bored. And so, on long car journeys, various strategies have to be adopted to keep them entertained. That's along with the perennial job of stopping them getting car sick, going to sleep on each other, and picking small fights.

"Mum, Isaac's gone to sleep on my shoulder..." is how they see it. Whereas you look back in the rear view mirror and see one of your kids resting their head on their older brother's shoulder and think, "Aw, sweet," all the elder child is thinking is, "Get them off me!"

Car games not only help solve the boredom of a long journey, they can help keep children's minds focused, so they don't go off to sleep when you don't want them to. Written like that it sounds slightly cruel, but any battle-weary parent will tell you that dozing off at the wrong moment can bring tears later on.

Growing up in England in the 60s and 70s, when the road system wasn't quite what it is today, meant long hauls to the West Country and to South Wales in the too-slow family car during the summer months. Playing car games with my parents and brother helped make the trip pass that much quicker—my dad was never into breaking any kind of speed limit, ever. A lot of the car games in the book are ones that I played as a child and have been handed down over the years. Then there are a few, like Bridge Baseball and Cow Football, that I've made up after extensive trials on my own unsuspecting children: Theo, Isaac, and Hetty.

There are a huge number of games that have been included in the book to cover almost every driving situation. Some of the games rely on busy roads with lots of vehicles around, some of them are best played on empty country roads where you pass few vehicles. Some need a regular supply of farm animals passing on either side of the car; others rely on traffic signals and the paraphernalia of the urban landscape to provide prompts for the games.

In the last few years the rise of in-car DVD players has bridged some of the boredom gap in keeping children entertained on the road, but they're far from a perfect solution. You end up coming from a house where the kids are hooked up to a screen, travel in a car where they're hooked up to a screen, and then when they arrive at the other end, they don't know what to do, save for finding another screen to watch with their friends. Car games are cheaper, far more interactive and help create children that know how to play and to entertain themselves, and are not struck dumb the second their life-support system of an LCD display is taken away.

Car games can tax their imagination, too. In the book there are a number of easy word games that you can play together to help pass the time, whether it's in the car, on the train, or delayed at an airport. So apart from having fun you can help enrich your children's vocabulary along the route. You might even be in for a surprise. My five-year-old daughter has come up with some astonishing words in a number of word games we play, which has left me thinking, "where on earth did she get that from?"

So, car journeys can also be a voyage of discovery with your children, they've certainly been the cause of some memorable family moments. Playing the impersonating animals game one time we had to stop the car because we were all—driver included—laughing so much. Trust me on this one, it was a very funny meerkat.

At the more worthy end of the car games spectrum I've included some learning and information games. These feature the kind of information I always get wrong in trivia quizzes such as the order of the planets in the solar system or the longest river in the world: I always say the Amazon, and it's always the Nile.

Throughout the book I haven't graded the various games as suitable for certain ages. Car games aren't like board games where you need to study the rules for half an hour before you can get started. You can work out in seconds whether a game is right for your children or not. Even mature twelve-year-olds who like to think of themselves as "really grown up now" like to play the silliest of games. At least they do in our family.

Finally, one of the great things about car games is that you can just make them up, quite literally, as you go along. If you want to adapt a game, do it. I've included a number of variations to each game, but you can go on refining and changing games to suit your own purposes.

I hope you enjoy *Car Games* and that playing them brings you as much fun as they've given my own family in the years we've been making car journeys.

Jo Pink
April 2004

It's easy to guess
which carriageway
we're on...

Spotting Games

The Animal Game

For the animal game, you split the car into two halves. The right-hand side of the car takes the right side of the road, and the left-hand side of the car takes the left.

This works well for a family of four, but it's up to parents how you split up three kids (or five) on the back seat.

Whenever you spot animals in fields on your side of the road you have to count them out loud. So if you pass them too quickly, before you've got to fifteen—too bad!

The winner is the side who has counted the most animals.

You can continue it in town, too, with domestic pets being walked or cats that dare to cross the street.

Variations

You can include birds kept in fields such as chickens, turkeys, or geese.

If you're passing through an area with few farm animals you can adapt it to any four-legged animals you see, provided you can shout out what they are.

Try including animals you see on billboards—again their names must be shouted out loud to score points.

Instead of counting the animals out loud, you can make mooing, baaing, or oinking noises. Great fun if there's more than one type of animal in the field!

License Plate Scramble

The idea of this game is to spot license plates from as many states as possible.

Depending on how well you and your kids travel, you can play the game a number of ways. Reading and writing on car journeys is best kept to a bare minimum to avoid carsickness, so pick the version most suitable for you.

Give them a clipboard and a pencil and ask them to write each different state name they spot on a license plate. No sharing of "spots!"

Set a time limit of half an hour or forty-five minutes. All "spots" have to be confirmed by an adult

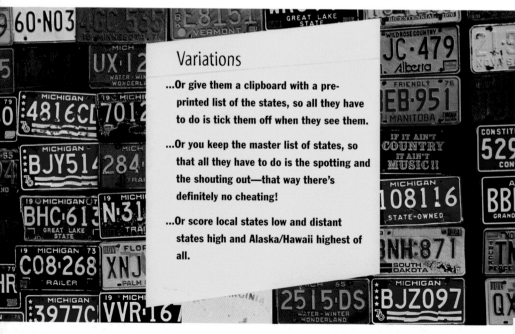

Variations

...Or give them a clipboard with a pre-printed list of the states, so all they have to do is tick them off when they see them.

...Or you keep the master list of states, so that all they have to do is the spotting and the shouting out—that way there's definitely no cheating!

...Or score local states low and distant states high and Alaska/Hawaii highest of all.

Sequences

License plates are a great source of game material. Apart from License Plate Scramble, they can be used to play "Sequences."

Get players to choose their own number sequence between 10 and 99—such as 23 or 65 or 79.

Once everyone has chosen their number, they have to spot it on a license plate. If someone has the number 23 then BHT 523 wins, but BHT 253 is not close enough.

Variations

Players can try and get from 1–20 or 1–50 using single numbers. One team could go from 1–20, the other from 20–1.

It's easy getting from 1–10, but from 11 onwards it gets tougher. This is a good game for the whole car to play together.

Red Car!

A game that Henry Ford never imagined would happen (his famous motto was, "you can have any color you like, providing it's black").

The Red Car game is simple. See who can spot a red car first. The person who spots it yells out, "Red car!" and gets a point. If they yell out "Red car!" and it's not, then it's minus a point.

Everyone has to see the red car for it to count.

Do maroon cars count?
Yes

Do half-red cars count?
Yes

Do red trucks count?
No

Do cars with a red stripe count?
It depends how big the stripe is.

Warning

Darker colors are a nightmare to adjudicate.

Variation

If you get bored of red, there's always blue, green, and yellow you can spot.

Dude, Where's My Orange Car?

If you want to give the kids something really difficult to do, ask them to spot an orange or a purple car. Orange may have been a big seller in the early 70s and 80s but ever since then cars in this color have hardly been out of a dealer's showroom.

Variation

Or you could add Orange Car to a list of rare vehicles, such as:

Ice cream van

Lumber truck

Hummer

Mobile crane

Boat on a transporter

Military vehicle

Glider in a trailer

Horse box

Road sweeper

Harvester

Motorcycle and sidecar

Alphabet Sequences

This game is just like the number sequences game, except that instead of using number sequence, the idea is to spot alphabet sequences. Again, it works best if the whole car plays as one team.

So, to start the game players need to spot the letter "A" on a license plate, then it's "BTY" or "BCM" or, if they're really lucky, "BCD" all on the same license plate.

However "BMC" would only count as the letter "B" (because the "B" and the "C" need to be next to each other—unless you want to play the game at lightning speed).

Variation

Split the car into two teams and have one team going backward through the alphabet, from Z to A, while the other is working forward, from A to Z. This works well as a race to finish spotting all the letters.

Special License Plates

Another license plate spotting game sets players the task of finding a variety of different things when they scan their eyes across the highway. You can play these games just for fun or give points each time someone spots one of the plates.

Words

Watch out for plates that spell out real words—no matter how short. There are endless three-letter examples, and quite a few short ones, too: IT, OR, OF, AS, AT, IS, TO, IF, US, UP, IN.

Remember, if you're playing for points, repeats aren't allowed!

words—for example THT, GNG or LYL will score.

Or you can try and spot number palindromes such as 121 or 848 or 999 or 2002.

Variation

You can play the games on this page singly, or you can combine them, depending on how much traffic is around at the time.

Palindromes

Palindromes are words that can be read the same backward, such as BOB or PIP. You can ask players to spot letter palindromes on license plates—they don't have to be real

Vanity Plates

There are lots of personalized number plates on the road these days—vehicle registrations that spell out a word. See if you can spot one.

Danger, Aggressive Carrot!

License Plate Phrases demands far more imagination than the other games.

Nominate a chooser to pick a passing car. They read out the license plate letters, such as DAC.

Then everybody has to instantly think of a three-word phrase starting with those three letters, such as: "Danger, Aggressive Carrot" or "Don't Argue, Caroline" or "Dogs and Cats."

The person who thinks up the best phrase gets a point.

Variations

The person who thinks up the phrase that makes the least sense is voted out.

Insist that nobody uses a name in their phrase.

Or insist that everybody has to use a name in their phrase.

Bus Stop Battle

There are loads of ways you can play games with people standing at bus stops. Providing you're not traveling past them too quickly, or you're on a Rocky Mountain pass or the Interstate!

Split the car into teams. One team takes the left side of the road, the other takes the right side of the road. Each time you pass a bus stop count the number of people waiting. The first team to reach 50 wins.

Variations

If you pass a bus stop with no one waiting then you delete one point from that team.

If there's an animal waiting at the bus stop they score 10 points.

Old ladies count two points—this can have everyone arguing so much that you can even miss bus stops. Some kids' idea of an old lady is anyone over 40!

I Spy

A classic car game—one player secretly spots something on view to everyone in the car and then the other players have to guess what it is. For the very few that don't already know it, the first player starts by saying...

"I spy with my little eye, something beginning with S..."

The player who guesses the object beginning with the letter "S" gets the next turn.

Except It's Not As Simple As That...

Dedicated I Spy players will know that it's very easy to spot something outside of the car that all of a sudden gets left miles behind. So when the answer is finally uncovered there are cries of, "So where was that, then?"

To make sure everyone knows what the score is, best to get players to add if it's "inside" or "outside" of the car.

That way, if it's outside, players can look around straight away.

That's My Car

A good game for a bunch of boys, or anyone who loves cars. This is also best played on a single carriageway.

Players pick a number from one to 100—but preferably with at least 10 in between each player (to help build the suspense). Then together everyone counts the cars that pass in the opposite direction.

The number that each player chooses, that is the player's pretend car. When all players have found their pretend car, the player who "picked" the most impressive vehicle wins.

Variations

Choosing "the most impressive car" can start arguments, so vary the game by picking a quality that is going to win. It could be the most luxurious car, the fastest car, the car that holds the most people, the cleanest car, the dirtiest car—you can make up whatever categories you like.

Playing Tips

Don't count trucks or anything else except cars. If it's a slow day with not much traffic on the road, count between one and 50. To avoid arguments over whose car is the winner, make sure an adult adjudicates.

That's Your Dream Car, That Is

This isn't so much a game, more a way of poking fun at anyone in the car—especially the grown-ups.

The idea is to spot the most rickety old wreck on four wheels and say, "That's your dream car, that is!"

It doesn't have to stop at cars, it can be anything. For instance, if the car's passing a tumbledown old shack at the side of the road, someone could shout, "That's your dream house, that is!"

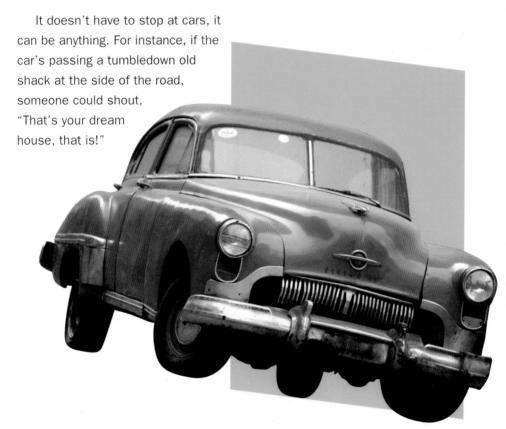

Stop Lights and Mailboxes

Stop Lights is a simple game best avoided on the freeway where players have to guess how many stoplights the car will go through on green before they get held up on red. All players guess at once and the person who gets closest to the right number wins.

Stop Lights and Mailboxes is a much more involved game, though. Each player takes it in turn to own the car and is trying to go through the most sets of stop lights on green.

If they hit a red light, their turn isn't necessarily ended, because each mailbox they spot between lights counteracts the next red. When a player runs out of mailboxes and is stopped by a red, it's the next player's turn. The winner is the player who's passed the most traffic lights.

Variations

This game can be played by the whole car or individual players.

You can carry over spare mailboxes from one set of lights to the next. If there are few mailboxes around on the streets, then a church or religious building can substitute.

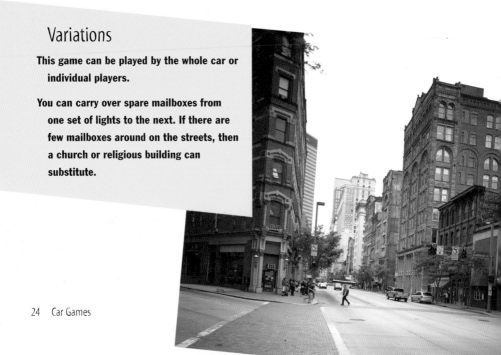

Two-doors and Vans versus Four-doors and SUVs

This is a game for single lane highways—play it on a multi-lane route and you've got yourself a sure-fire headache.

One player or team counts the number of two-door cars and vans that pass by, going in the opposite direction. One player or team counts four-door cars and SUVs.

You can set a mileage limit with the odometer, or a time limit. Or, as in a lot of car games, a fed-up-with-this-game limit.

Variation

You can vary the vehicles to give one team a whole range of different things to look out for. So you can end up with:

Team A: Two-doors, vans, motorhomes, trucks

Team B: Four-doors, SUVs, big rigs and motorbikes

Playing Tips

You can assess the score as the game unfolds and do a little bit of leveling to keep things interesting. For instance, if four-doors are winning by a mile you can suddenly remember the rule that, "If a car is towing a caravan, boat, or trailer that's minus 10 points."

Bridge Baseball

Bridge baseball is a great game to play on the motorway in built-up areas where there are few animals to count, but loads of bridges.

It helps a lot if you know the rules of baseball, but for those who don't, the basic rule is that a player has to get round four bases before he/she gets back home to score a point.

There's no pitching side, everybody bats. There's also no stopping at a base. Once a player starts he has to keep on going.

The batting player waits for the first bridge to come along. If there is any form of human or four-legged animal life (birds don't count) on the bridge, then he/she gets to first base. The people can be in a car, on a bike, in a bus, or just crossing on foot, it doesn't matter which.

If there are no vehicles, or any sign of human life clearly crossing the bridge, that player is o-u-t, OUT! And the next player is in to bat.

The player at first base moves on to second base providing there's someone on bridge number two. Exactly the same rules apply, if something is either on or crossing the bridge they're in. If there's no one to be seen, they're out.

Tension rises after third base. Will they get to score…? Four bridges in a row with people, cars, or animals crossing scores a point and that player then takes a rest and it's someone else's turn.

Cow Football!

Like the Animal Game the car is split into two teams and each team takes one side of the road.

Again the teams are looking out for farm animals: sheep, horses, pigs, and cows.

The big difference is that this time the scoring system is based on pro-football scoring.

1–2 animals in a field = 2 points:
  Safety!

3–9 animals in a field = 3 points:
  Field Goal!

10+ animals in a field = 6 points:
  Touchdown!

Plus, the team gets an extra point after their touchdown—a Point After—if:
* One of the animals is a completely different color
* One of them is lying down
* One has a youngster suckling as you drive past.

Variations

The teams can impose a two minute Time Out if they suspect the car is about to drive past a big field of animals that will benefit their rivals. During the Time Out no points can be scored.

• Time Outs cannot be called while you are driving past a field of animals, they must be called before.

• Four Time Outs per journey; only one can be called in the last ten minutes.

• Of course if you want all hell to break loose you can allow Time Outs to be taken mid-field, but expect some ructions.

For added reality you can split the game into four 15-minute quarters.

Treasure Hunt

The Treasure Hunt game needs a small amount of preparation before you set off on your journey. For each child construct a list of 10 things they have to spot on the journey. You can incentivize them with a chocolate-per-object-spotted scheme.

Each child has their own list and a pencil so they can cross off each item as they spot it through the trip.

The kind of things to watch out for will vary depending on what kind of countryside or urban landscape you're heading through. A cactus plant might be a good thing to spot in New Mexico but certainly not in New England.

Here's some ideas of things you might include:

Fir tree

Dead tree

Fire engine

Ambulance

Police patrol

Bird of prey

Sea bird

Sheep

Pig

Horse

Pink car

Orange car

Saint Bernard dog

German shepherd dog

Mustang

Corvette

Railway bridge over a river

Goods train

Passenger train

Greyhound bus

School bus

Burger King

McDonalds

Taco Bell

Ford showroom

General Motors showroom

Roadside vegetable stall

Cinema

Theater

Church with a tower

Church with a steeple

Motel

Hotel

Holiday Inn

Days Inn

So, What Am I Counting?

One player decides to count something outside of the car. It could be street lights, telegraph poles, green signs, single-story houses, ponds, dogs, or roadkill. What they don't do is tell anyone what it is they're counting.

Instead, whenever they pass the object they've selected, whether it's a light/pole/sign/pond, they count out loud, adding to their score.

The other players have to guess what it is that's being counted.

Playing Tips

To keep the game moving, ask players not to choose really rare things to spot—such as piebald horses, juggling sheep or houses with a ladder on the roof.

Variation

If the object a player has chosen doesn't appear within the next three miles then they lose their go.

Guessing Games

Silent Counting

How long does a second last? The time it takes to say "one thousand" or even "one elephant?"

Here's the challenge. Ask someone in the car to count out a minute silently in their heads. At the same time, someone with a second hand on their watch keeps note of the time. When the player thinks they've reached a minute they shout out, "NOW!"

How many seconds are they off their target minute? Try it again with everyone in the car and see who can get closest.

Variation

Two, three or even four players can play this at once with everyone shouting out when they think the minute is up.

If you have three or more players give everyone a separate word to shout, otherwise you won't know who's shouted out closest to the minute mark, whilst keeping your eyes glued to your watch!

Bing Who? (or The Bing Game)

This is a game that splits the car in two. This one is grown-ups versus children. And the grown-ups' decision is final.

The basic version of the game is as follows: the children or teenagers in the car have to shout out a first name and the grown-ups have to think of a famous person with that name.

They can be celebs, sports stars, fictional characters from books, television and movies, or even relations.

For every person the grown-ups name, they get a point—for every person they fail to name the children get a point.

Variation

Grown-ups, give yourselves five Time Outs for when the little rascals think up something fiendish, if you want to stack the odds in your favor.

Because the game requires a good knowledge of famous people, children are at a disadvantage in doing the naming, but they can always play among themselves if they are evenly matched.

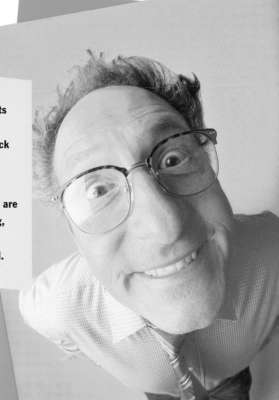

Backseat Hide and Seek

Let's be honest, there aren't that many places to hide in the back seat of the car, especially when everyone has seatbelts on.

Car Games hide and seek involves a lot more imagination than the real-life version. One player thinks of a good hiding place in their house or garden. The rest of the car has to find out where that is by asking a series of questions.

All the "hiding player" must answer is yes or no. So the interrogation could proceed along the lines of:

Are you outside? **No**

Are you inside? **Yes**

Are you upstairs? **Yes**

Are you in the loft? **No**

Are you in the bathroom? **No**

The object of the game is to find the player with the fewest number of questions as possible.

Playing Tips

The player who's hiding has to find a place that is out of sight if someone were to walk into the room in real life. They can't be sitting at a desk or just standing to one side of the door.

They have to physically fit into the place described, give or take a few inches. Players can't get away with picking a place that only a small hamster would fit into.

Who Am I?

Like *Backseat Hide And Seek*, this game revolves around smart guesswork and asking the right questions.

One player chooses a person that they know, and, most importantly, that the other passengers in the car know. They don't reveal who it is.

Now it is up to the rest of the players to ask a series of questions that reveal their identity.

All the choosing player must answer is yes or no. So the interrogation could proceed along the lines of:

Is it a male?   **Yes**

Is he Mom and Dad's age?   **Yes**

Is he a teacher at school?   **No**

Has he been to our house?   **Yes**

Is he one of Dad's friends?   **Yes**

There are bound to be a few questions that come up for which the chooser doesn't know the precise answer, so they can be allowed to give an approximate answer sometimes: "I think so" and "sort of" and so on.

Variations

Start by playing with people known to the family then branch out into pop stars, sports stars, and movie stars.

Or even have a game based exclusively on cartoon characters.

If you have good questioners who can think up lots of quick questions, let players ask a series of questions till they get a "no".

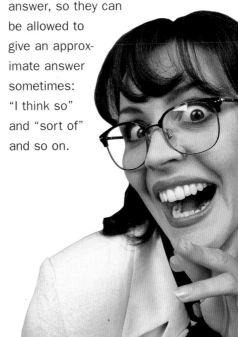

What Am I?

A game very similar to *Who Am I?* but this time use things instead of people.

A player chooses a real-life object and the rest have to guess what it is by asking a series of questions for which the answer is either "yes" or "no."

Unlike the previous game, this version demands a much more detailed level of questioning, because "the thing" could be a lawn mower, a hockey pitch, an aircraft carrier, or a donut.

Variations

Instead of choosing an object, choose an animal, fish, bird, or insect. Or how about a plant of some kind?

There is a similar sort of game known as Hidden In My Room. The first player secretly chooses an object then says, "Hidden in my room is something that is *small...*" and the missing word is an adjective that describes the object, such as "small," "furry," "smelly," or "black."

It would be a real lucky guess to hit on the right answer in one, so the players then get another chance when the chooser adds another description.

"Hidden in my room is something that is *small* and *circular*" and if no one guesses, the chooser keeps on adding clues until it is patently obvious what it is.

You can allow all sorts of things to be hidden in a bedroom that wouldn't normally fit, all the way from a lawn mower to a nuclear power station.

Speed, Distance, Time

These *guesstimation* games are all to do with the car journey.

Speed

Ask everyone in the car to close their eyes for 30 seconds (apart from the driver). Don't say what the game is going to be until everyone has their eyes well and truly shut. Then everyone has to use the sound and vibration from the car to work out how fast it's traveling.

Guesses must be made before eyes are opened again.

Time

Make a note of what time you set off, then after you've gone over half distance, ask everybody how long you've been on the road.

Distance

If you've zeroed the odometer before you start, at the same time as you're asking how long the journey's taken, you can ask how far you've traveled.

Or, spot a landmark on the horizon that you know you'll be traveling by. Everyone has to guess how many miles it will be till you pass it.

Spoof

This game needs everyone to have three coins in their hand; they can be pennies, dimes, whatever, their value is not important—they can even be non-sticky candies (see below).

You all put your hands behind your backs and secretly select whether you are going to keep zero, one, two, or three coins in the hand you put forward.

With your other hand behind your back, present the hand with the coins, without revealing its contents. The aim of the game is to guess how many coins are hidden. This will depend on how many are playing. For example, if there are four people there could be a maximum of 12 coins and a minimum of zero.

One player starts off by estimating how many coins are hidden in total in all the hands. The first player calls out a number and everyone guesses a number in turn, making sure not to repeat someone else's number.

Once everyone has selected their number, the hands are revealed and the real number of coins is counted. The person who was closest to the total drops out. If it's a tie with two players, one number either side, then the round is null and void.

Play resumes, with the person to the left of the person who started in the first round guessing first, until the ultimate loser is the last person in.

Variations

If you want to use the game as a way of getting your kids to learn to count money, you can count up the value of all the coins and instead of asking everyone to guess the number of coins, guess the value of coins in each round.

With a smaller number of people in the circle, use more coins to make things interesting.

Abstract Questions

It's a line of questioning you often see posed in magazine interviews when a celebrity is asked, "If you were a car, what kind of car would you be?"

It's usually meant to draw out a light-hearted or wacky response—for cars you can be fast and sporty, or you can be big and practical, or even luxurious and graceful.

Applying the same logic to a game, one player has to choose a person who they know very well. The other players must also know this person well and they have to guess who it is by asking a series of abstract questions.

For example:

If this person was a tree, what would it be?

If this person was an animal, what would it be?

If this person was a kind of weather, what would it be?

If this person was an emotion, what would it be?

If this person was a piece of clothing, what would it be?

If this person was a flavor of ice cream, what would it be?

Questions continue until someone gets the right answer.

Playing Tips

Before you start it's a good idea to limit your choices to a specific area, such as celebrities, athletes, fictional characters, people you know, etc.

To prevent the guessers getting sidetracked by misleading answers, the person answering can dodge the occasional question for which there is no obvious answer. Otherwise the guessers might be sent down a false trail.

To aid the guessers, the chooser can add clues into the answers.

The Next Car Will Be...

This is a game for wandering country roads, or winding mountain roads. Or just not very busy roads.

Players guess the color of the next car to come past them in the opposite direction—white, green, gray, red, blue, etc, everyone with their own separate color. There's a point for each correct guess.

Set a mileage on the car's odometer to determine the finishing line.

Variation

Instead of using colors of cars, you could pick different types of vehicle that are going to come round the bend toward you. Because cars are going to be the most common vehicles you can give higher points to other vehicles

Trucks: 2 points

Pick-ups: 2 points

SUVs: 3 points

Mini vans: 3 points

Car with trailer: 5 points-

Tractor or farm vehicle: 12 points

Police car: 20 points

Name That Beaten Out Tune

This one is a tried and tested favorite on car journeys. Instead of humming or playing a familiar TV theme tune, players have to beat out the tune against a car seat or anything that will make a noise: legs, containers, but not a brother or sister!

Providing the tune is within the experience of the players, such as children's programs like *The Simpsons* and *The Muppets*, it should be recognizable.

Some tunes that are normally recognized within 10 seconds:

The Muppets

The Simpsons

The Addams Family

Rugrats

Variation

You can try humming if the rhythm of the tune isn't a big enough clue.

Playing Tips

With older children you can move on to films or even pop songs, but it's best not to try too wide a range of subjects or you'll be guessing all day, followed by the bitter accusations: "That didn't sound anything like (insert name of song here)" or, "I've never heard of that."

* For the older, more complicated tunes, a clue or two might be necessary.

* Keep the guessing down to a narrow field—such as cartoons, Disney film songs, No.1 hits, nursery rhymes etc.

Action Games

Stone, Scissors, Paper

Another classic game that can be played in the car, on the plane, or wherever boredom strikes.

This is a game for two players who each make a sign with their hand at exactly the same time—the signs are either **stone**, **scissors**, or **paper**.

Stone is a clenched fist, **scissors** is a closed palm with the index and middle finger forming a "V," like the open blades of a pair of scissors, and for **paper**, hold the palm open and flat.

Players keep their hand behind their back and then count, 1–2–3 and on 3, both players reveal which sign they have chosen to see who wins the round.

Paper beats **stone**, because paper can wrap round stone. **Stone** beats **scissors**, because a stone will blunt a pair of scissors, and **scissors** beats **paper**, because scissors cut paper.

If players both choose the same sign it's a draw. Play as many rounds as you like.

Playing Tip

Make sure there aren't any last-second changes of hand signals.

Waving

It's fun to wave from the car when you're little. And people love to wave back.

A good game for a multi-lane highway, see how many waves you can get back in the space of half an hour.

Waving is good, smiling is great, but making faces is out. Especially if you're driving.

A game for the very young, you can get the kids to wave and teach them how to count (how many waves they get back) at the same time.

Waving Chicken

This is a game for long, empty roads with few cars about. It was told to me by someone who traveled a lot in Australia, where in the more remote parts, passing another car is a real event. The same could apply to the vast empty spaces of Texas, the Rockies, or even the highlands of Scotland.

In Australia, when cars do pass each other, it's quite common for the occupants of cars to wave to each other.

The most obvious "waver" is the person in the passenger seat, the rest of the players in the car instruct them whether to wave or not. As another car approaches, a decision has to be made—do we wave or do we chicken out of waving?

If you wave and you get a wave back, that's a point.

If you wave and you don't get a wave back, that's a minus point.

If you decide not to wave and you don't get a wave, that's also a point.

But if you decide not to wave and the other car waves at you first, then that's the ultimate failure—two minus points!

The skill apparently is working out what kind of car is coming toward you and whether the occupants of that kind of car or truck is likely to wave or not.

Playing Tip

Don't try this on an Interstate.

Noises

Whoever has hold of this book reads out a noise from the list below and the player has to name an object or animal that makes the noise. Or add some of your own favorite noise words to the list.

click	clank	rattle	slam
eek	needeep	ding	splurge
splosh	bong	ding-dong	gurgle
tic-toc	crash	woof	toot
plop	ooze	miaow	hoot
boom	squeak	tap	parp
bang	creak	woosh	moo
click	slurp	neigh	honk
roar	bonk	bray	glug
tweet	crinkle	oink	whistle
honk	crackle	slurp	whine
clonk	rustle	tinkle	whinny

Invent your own points scoring system as to who made the most convincing, least convincing, loudest, quietest, most gruesome noise.

Expressions

If you have a potential drama queen in the family, this is where they can take center stage.

One person names an extreme emotion and one player has to make a face that expresses it. Some good faces to act out are:

Happy

Ecstatic

Sad

Miserable

Worried

Frightened

Petrified

Grumpy

Angry

Puzzled

Suspicious

Jealous

Loving

Sleepy

Sparky

Evil

Goody-goody

Disgusted

Thoughtful

Intimidated

Guilty

Variation

Get the person who chooses the emotion to whisper it in the actor's ear and then the other people in the car have to guess what it is.

Mimes

There's more acting required in the mime game. One player has to act out an action, such as cleaning teeth, sending an email, or taking a photograph, and the other players have to guess what it is.

Here are some ideas to get you going:

Cleaning shoes

Using the phone

Throwing a basketball

Putting on a coat

Painting a wall

Eating a banana

Using the microwave

Flying a kite

Writing a letter (don't forget the envelope and stamp)

Putting on sunglasses

Variations

Be an animal—this one can have the car in fits of laughter (certainly my meerkat had such an uproarious reaction we had to stop the vehicle once, not because it was a great impression either, the driver just couldn't stop laughing).

Without telling the rest of the car what they are, players have to mime popular, distinctive animals, from moles to meerkats, from kangaroos to koalas. Importantly, players are not allowed to use any sound effects whatsoever. They can use their hands, for instance; to act out a cat licking its paws and cleaning its fur, or to show how big their ears are.

Playing Tip

Start with very easy, simple actions before moving on to the more difficult variations.

Quietest in the Car

While a lot of the other car games challenge and excite the occupants of the back seats, this is one that calms everything down.

From the moment the signal is given everyone has to be as quiet as possible. The winner is the one who keeps quietest for the longest time.

Not Allowed

* *Humming*

* *Coughing loudly*

* *Distracting fellow competitors*

* *Tickling other competitors*

Parents' Note

This is often a great way to get younger children off to sleep. Our five-year-old daughter not only keeps very quiet, she also keeps very still and frequently drops off to sleep trying her hardest to win.

Warning

If it's night time, make sure everyone's been to the bathroom, just in case of those little accidents...

Don't Laugh!

For this game players have to withstand all the efforts of the rest of the car to get them to laugh and they have a minute to do it. They have to keep an absolutely straight face throughout.

To heighten the pressure and give it a big build-up, it's best if Mom or Dad can give it an unnecessarily long introduction. Something on the lines of: "Right, this is Isaac's turn at being absolutely silent. He's not going to laugh, giggle, or even smile in the next minute. He's going to keep exactly the same expression on his face...and he's not going to say a single word, either. He's just going to look very, very serious."

Then when the clock starts, all the others can pull faces or do what they like to try and get Isaac to laugh. Except they can't touch him in any way.

Variation

Another great version of this game is to give the player with the "poker face" a nonsense phrase that they have to use as the answer to any question that is thrown at them. For example, the answer he or she is given might be, "43 melons and a fly swatter."

The rest of the car then ask the player questions, such as, "What are you sitting on?" to which the answer must always be, "43 melons and a fly swatter," said with a perfectly straight face.

Just wait for it to crumple...

Imagination Games

Weird Vacations

Everyone can have fun planning a weird vacation with this nonsense game. Players have to make up a sentence about where they're going on holiday, who they're going with and what they're going to do when they get there. The only limiting factor is they all have to begin with the same letter.

The destination, the person (or thing) they're going with and their activity must begin with the same letter. For example:

I'm off to Paris with a parrot to pick poppies.

I'm off to Iceland with an iguana to idle about in an igloo.

I'm off to Zanzibar with Zoe to zoom around a zoo.

Playing Tip

If you allow names to be used, limit players to people they know in real life.

Don't Finish the Sentence

This game is sometimes known as the never-ending sentence. Players have to continue a sentence that someone else starts, but never quite bring it to a natural period.

Here's an example:

Player 1 ...I went to the doctor's on Friday, but...

Player 2 ...I couldn't find the right door to go in, so...

Player 3 ...I asked a man in the car park, who said...

Player 4 ...I'd probably come a day early, and...

Player 1 ...it wasn't a good idea to...

The longer the sentence goes on, the more complicated and convoluted it becomes, but no matter how tempting, the players must never end the sentence.

And players are NOT allowed to leave the sentence hanging with the same linking word that others have used in the sentence.

The game ends when someone either duplicates a linking word or their words make no sense at all.

...I went to the doctors on Friday, but...

...I couldn't find the right door to go into, so...

...It wasn't a good idea to...

...I asked a man in the carpark, who said...

...I'd probably come a day early, and...

Knock, Knock Jokes

Knock, knock jokes never cease to amuse children who will try and make up their own, whether you like it or not.

Here's what you can do just with the letter "A"

Knock, knock

Who's there?

Adelia!

Adelia who?

Adelia the cards and we'll play snap!

Knock, knock

Who's there?

Aardvark!

Aardvark who?

Aardvark on the pavement!

Knock, knock

Who's there?

Adolf!

Adolf who?

Adolf ball hit me in da dose.

Knock, knock

Who's there?

Alaska!

Alaska who?

Alaska my friend the question then!

Knock, knock

Who's there?

Aladdin!

Aladdin who?

Aladdin the street wants a word with you.

Knock, knock

Who's there?

Albert!

Albert who?

Albert you don't know who this is.

Knock, knock

Who's there?

Alec!

Alec who?

Alec my lolly, but you can't!

Knock, knock

Who's there?

Alfred!

Alfred who?

Alfred the needle if you sew!

Knock, knock

Who's there?

Andrew!

Andrew who?

Andrew a picture!

Knock, knock

Who's there?

Annie!

Annie who?

Annie one you like!

Knock, knock

Who's there?

Arthur!

Arthur who?

Arthur any more sweets in Mom's bag?

Knock, knock

Who's there?

Athena!

Athena who?

Athena flying thaw-ther (saucer)!

And They All Lived Happily Ever After...

In this game, each player has to think up the ending to a fairy story. But it's not a well-known fairy story. The narrator starts off an original, improvised tale and builds up a few well-defined characters—knights, dragons, goblins, castles, princesses, witches, wizards, etc.—over the space of two or three minutes.

The story is paused with the characters in some kind of predicament. It's then the job of the other players in the car to try and provide the best solution or ending to the story which, as in all fairy stories, should have the hero and heroine living happily ever after.

Players vote to see which ending they think is the best.

Variations

This doesn't have to be too challenging for younger children if you begin a story with characters they know from their own books and videos.

Of course it doesn't have to be fairy stories, but it's best to start off with a story-telling format that children are familiar with. From fairy stories, the wide world of literature is open to you. Just don't try *War and Peace*!

Car Poetry

Have a go at creating some car poetry on the move. If they're just five lines long then you won't have to write them down to remember them. One we created is published below.

Limericks are great fun and you can build them up line by line. For example:

A beautiful princess called Hetty

Had fallen in love with spaghetti

She loved it so much

She loved even the touch

But the mess on her dress wasn't pretty

Each player can suggest a line of the limerick, or alternatively, build it up line by line together, agreeing which is the best next line as it is constructed, before moving onto the next one.

Variations

A more artistic form of poetry can be Five-Senses Poetry or Five-Color Poetry. With Five-Senses Poetry, each line is about a different sense—touch, sight, sound, smell, and taste, all relating to the same subject.

The sight of my dog makes me happy

The smell of my dog is so doggy

The touch of my dog is furry and wet

The sound of my dog is woof, woof woof

But the taste of my dog is NEVER!

With Five-Color Poetry, each line is about a different color.

A rose is as red as blood

The sea is as blue as my pyjamas

The grass is a green space I play on

The fire glows orangey bright

Dad's face is as black as a thunder cloud

Just a Minute!

This is very similar to *And They All Lived Happily Ever After*, except this is a game for the whole car to play together. A narrator starts off a story and builds up a storyline for the rest of the players to follow.

It's then the job of all the players to take turns in developing the story for a minute before passing it over.

The story can go round and round getting more and more bizarre until the narrator decides to bring it to a close.

Variations

Insist that each player has to kill off one character and introduce a new one in their minute of story-telling.

Or how about every player needing to include the same unusual word or phrase in their minute of story telling—such as clogs, clarinet, or cliff top?

So, What If...?

An imagination game, this one gives children the sense of what might be, what could be, if they think BIG enough.

So, what if you could have any superhero superpower?

What would it be?

So, what if you could load up a trolley in the toy store for free?

What three things would you pick?

So, what if you could go on vacation anywhere in the world?

Where would you go?

So, what if you could skip two lessons at school?

What subjects would they be?

So, what if you had a pop star put on a special concert for you and your friends?

Who would you choose?

So, what if you could have any pet?

What animal would you pick?

So, what if you could be a guest star in a top TV series?

Which one would it be?

So, what if your lottery numbers came up?

What would you blow $10m on?

So, what if you could travel back in time?

How far would you go?

So, what if you could become invisible?

What would you do?

So, what if you could meet anyone from history?

Who would it be?

So, what if they made you into a cartoon character?

Which series would you want to appear in?

My Favorite Things

This is a game not played for points, but to find out what everybody likes about any subject imaginable.

Someone names a subject and each player in turn has to name their favorite; it could be breakfast cereal, desert, sport, subject at school, fast food, anything.

To help you along here are a list of subjects:

animals	times of day	games	names
car games	seasons	shoes	dances
cereals	fast foods	teachers	hobbies
clothes	books	cousins	drinks
vacations	films	funfair rides	pop stars
sports	records	friends	toys
cartoons	pets	jokes	smells
TV programs	flowers	characters	shops

Variations

How about bringing in the "Yuck!" factor and getting people to name their least favorite things.

Alternatively, if players in the car know each other very well, they could try and guess what other people's favorite things are.

Five Things/Ten Things is a tried and tested way of finding out how much your kids know. Ask them to name five trees, five fish, or five ways of keeping the rain off and see how long it takes them. For older children give them a list of ten. The sky's the limit as far as subject matter is concerned.

When I Went on Holiday I Remembered to Pack...

This is a favorite old game that people know in many different forms. Basically, it's a game about remembering a very long list. Or, if you're bad at it, forgetting a very short one.

A player starts with the sentence: **"When I went on holiday I remembered to pack...*a toothbrush.*"**

The next player could add, for example, toothpaste. So they say: "When I went on holiday I remembered to pack a toothbrush and some toothpaste."

The next player adds another item to the list. "When I went on holiday I remembered to pack a toothbrush, some toothpaste, and my pet iguana called Alfonse." Gradually, the list grows until someone is bound to get the sequence wrong.

And then they're out.

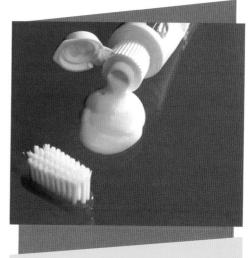

Variation

Personalize it with: Coming back from _____ (wherever you've just been to) I saw... And make players add things they really have seen or visited during the trip.

Word Games

The Nasty Butterfly...

This is less of a competitive game and more of an exercise in thinking up words and showing children the sheer power of adjectives. The idea of the game is to think up two words you would never find written together, unless it was in some tall tale or nonsense poem.

Using words out of context can create some fantastic, imagination-stretching word pictures for kids.

You can make boring words sound interesting or you can make exciting words sound boring. It teaches children the fun—and power—they can have with words.

Make Boring Things Sound Interesting

exploding headmaster

friendly wall

comfortable brick

rubbery library

Make Animals Sound Weird

hairy dolphin

seasick squid

intellectual ape

beautiful flea

Make Exciting Things Sound Boring

lonely disco

slimy birthday cake

miserable cartoon

sleepy roller-coaster

Opposites

A word game to challenge players' vocabulary and also their understanding of the meaning of words.

One person says a word, then the other has to find the antonym or opposite. Everyone starts with ten points and you lose a point for each time you can't find an opposite. The winner is the last one left in.

Happy/Sad

Brave/Cowardly

Strong/Weak

Loud/Quiet

Positive/Negative

Big/Small

Massive/Minute

Smelly/Odorless

Hard/Easy

Brilliant/Dull

Love/Hate

Narrow/Wide

Good/Bad

Ugly/Handsome

Tall/Short

Playing Tip

Don't let players get away with adding "un" on the front of words.

The Ticking Bomb

This game is another that requires a license plate to start it off. First, the chooser finds a plate with a letter sequence that is commonly found in a lot of different words.

For instance from the plate YEN 569 the chooser takes the letters EN. It's then the players' job to take it in turn to shout out a word with those two letters in, such as: Tent, When, Spend, Lend, Bend, Friend, Rent, Entertainment, etc.

If they can't think of something, it's up to the other players to count them down 5-4-3-2-1—Bang! And the ticking bomb explodes.

That person then gets a point and at the end of the game the person with the least points wins. Anyone who repeats a word that's already been suggested, loses the round and gets a point.

Playing Tip

This game can be shaped by whoever chooses the letters—so if younger players are involved, use simpler letter combinations and for older players, more difficult ones.

Rhyming Bomb

Like the ticking bomb, players take it in turn to shout out a word. This time, though, it's not prompted by a license plate.

Someone starts with a word of their choice—for example, "Sally," this is followed by "Rally," "Tally," "Pally," "Alley..."

Or perhaps: "Card," "Guard," "Shard," "Lard," "Hard," "Starred," "Sparred," "Barred."

If a player is stuck they get a 5-4-3-2-1 countdown before the explosion. The losing player gets to choose the next word that has to be rhymed.

The Bong Game
(Don't Say No/Don't Say Yes)

This is a fun game to play over a short amount of time. One person in the car has to answer questions about themselves for a minute without saying no or yes. The second they say "no" or "yes" they're given the gong—Bong!—and they're out.

What's your name?

Michael

Your name's Michael is it?

That's right

You're nine?

Eight

Eight?

Yes

Bong!

Variation

Instead of using the words "yes" or "no" as the banned words you can nominate a different word that people mustn't say in conversation. Make it a common word that crops up in a lot of sentences, such as "the," "and," or, "but." Then ask someone a lot of questions which they have to answer without using it.

Playing Tips

To make sure there's no cheating, you need to make sure that players stick strictly to the rules:

* Players must answer straight away, if they pause they can be bonged.

* Players must answer correctly. If they shout out any old information in answer to the question then they can be bonged.

* Players have to answer differently every time. They can't answer the same way twice. For instance, the older and smarter ones could try and use, "that's right" or "that's wrong" for "no" and "yes."

For an answer used twice they'll get the inevitable "Bong!"

Backward Spelling

Another great game to teach word awareness. One player thinks of a word, then, without revealing what it is, begins to spell it out loud. Except they start with the last letter first and proceed to spell the word backward.

The other players in the car have to work out what the word is going to be. The first person to guess and shout out correctly wins the next go.

So car becomes: R-A-C

Fun becomes: N-U-F

Cloud becomes: D-U-O-L-C

Games becomes: S-E-M-A-G

Playing Tip

Start with three- or four-letter words to get into the swing of things. To help players guess the words early, you can limit the subject area to particular themes—such as animals, plants, or means of transport.

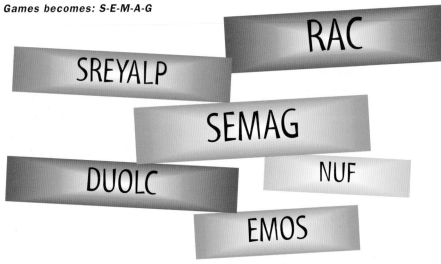

Compound Words and Phrases

This game is like a relay race for words with the baton being handed on each time. A compound word is a long word made out of two shorter words. Players have to form a word or phrase using the second word of a compound word or phrase.

A player starts with a word such as "Cargo" (car and go).The next player has to find a word or phrase beginning with "Go."

So the sequence could progress:

Cargo—Go-Kart—

Cartwheel—Wheelhouse—

Housewife...

Playing Tip

Don't limit yourself to actual compound words or you're unlikely to get anywhere. Two-word phrases such as "Skipping rope" are fine.

carGO – GO-kart

go-KART – CARTwheel

cartWHEEL – WHEELhouse

wheelHOUSE – HOUSEwife

Verb and Noun Tennis

This game is based on words that are both nouns and verbs.

Players take it in turn to shout out a verb that is also a noun. So the sequence could go something like this:

Stamp—Load—Train—Log—Spell— Dive—Hop—Leap—Jump

The aim of the game is to keep a "rally" going as long as possible, and the more players in the circle, the more thinking time.

Variation

If you get really good at this game, you could even throw in an alphabetical sequence, so players have to think of a noun/verb with the letter "A" and then "B" and so on. Players can count forward the sequence of letters and anticipate which letter they'll be getting next.

The Janitor's Dog

The janitor's dog is an Awful dog.
The janitor's dog is an Awesome dog.
The janitor's dog is an Amiable dog.
The janitor's dog is an Aggressive dog.

For this game you have to find an adjective beginning with a certain letter. In this case we've used the letter "A," but it might just as well be the letter "C" or "D" (but probably not "X" or "Z").

Players take it in turn to find an adjective for the dog beginning with the letter "A" until someone repeats an adjective or gets stuck. That person is then out and the rest move on to another letter. The last person standing is the winner.

Variations

It's so easy to personalize this game. It doesn't have to be the janitor's dog or the farmer's horse; it could be your aunt's bathrobe or the mayor's tree.

Also, to make things a little more specific, you can choose positive adjectives or negative adjectives or even energetic adjectives.

Alphabets

For this game players have to rack their brains for words on a particular theme. But they're not allowed to use just any words, they have to be words beginning with a certain letter of the alphabet.

Someone starts the game off by naming a category. For instance:

Animals	Cities	Drinks	Girls' names
Birds	Clothes	Fish	Movies
Books	Computer games	Flowers	Occupations
Boys' names		Foods	Rivers and States
Cars	Countries	Fruit and vegetables	Song titles
Cartoons	Dogs	Furniture (and things round the house)	Towns
		Games	TV shows
			Sports

Variations

Cold places on the planet

Hot places on the planet

Cold things

Hot things

Horrible food

Silly (anything that is thought of as silly)

Anything beginning with the letter "Q"

Anything beginning with the letter "Z"

Then someone else chooses the letter. Players take it in turns to name things from that category. Every time they think of something with the correct letter they put one finger (or thumb) up. If players can't think of something when it's their go, they drop out—and they're not allowed back in.

Synonyms

For this game players have to find a group of words that all have the same sort of meaning—words that carry a similar meaning are called synonyms.

One player starts the game off by choosing a word such as "tired." The next player has to think of a word with a similar meaning, for example "fatigued," the next player might think up "weary," and the next thinks up "exhausted."

Or the sequence could run: "shout," "yell," "scream," "roar," "cry," "howl," "bawl."

The game keeps on going until a player cannot think of one more word with a similar meaning, or they think of something that is not close enough, in this instance it could be words like "asleep" or "bored," which have a connection but don't really mean the same thing.

Playing Tip

Keep the words as simple as you can to start off with.

Lovers of Extreme Car Games could even bring their own mini *Roget's Thesaurus* with them.

Variations

To help the game along you can allow two word phrases—for the above example it would be something like "puffed out" or "worn out."

Letter Word Tag

You can play this game with all kinds of different word categories or themes. Someone decides the category, for example, "Geography." The first player picks a word such as "Caribbean" and then the second player has to name a geography-related word starting with the end letter of that word.

In this example it's the letter N, so it could be Namibia, or Nova Scotia, or Norway, or New Orleans.

The following player has to quickly think up a destination beginning with the last letter of Namibia, and so on until someone becomes stuck and is bonged out. Start everyone off with ten points and deduct a point every time they get "bonged."

Variations

How about three-letter word tag and four-letter word tag, but on any subject you like.

For more themes or categories see Alphabets on page 70.

Rhyming Celebs

Rhyming slang is used by Londoners every day of the week and you can use it in a car game. Cockney rhyming slang substitutes a small phrase for a word, for example the phrase "mutt and jeff" means "deaf." This is a chance to make up your own rhyming slang.

Here are some more:

Apples and pears = stairs

Mince pies = eyes

Tom and Dick = sick

Dog and bone = phone

Pen and ink = stink

In this game, players invent a phrase, and the end word has to rhyme with a celebrity's name. The other players in the car have to work out who the celebrity is. For example: No need to push, it's...? The answer is George W. Bush.

She's got massive ears—it's Britney Spears

He's so scary—it's Jim Carey

He's in the know—it's Russell Crowe

He likes a snooze—it's Tom Cruise

She loves her fiancé—it's Beyoncé

DropOut

This is a crafty word construction game that involves a bit of bluffing.

Like the never-ending sentence game, the idea is not to finish a word off. One player starts off with the first letter of a word, the second player adds a second letter, and so on—everyone who adds a letter must have an end word in mind, though they don't have to reveal it unless challenged. The letter they add mustn't complete a word.

For example:

Player 1: "H"

Player 2: "O"—they're thinking of the word "home"

Player 3: "S"—they're thinking of the word "host" (and "hos" isn't a word)

Player 4: "P"—they're thinking of the word "hospital" (and "hosp" isn't a word)

Player 1: "I"—they're thinking of the word "hospice or hospital" (and "hospi" isn't a word)

Player 2: "T"—they're thinking of the word "hospital" too and realize that Player 4 is going to get stuck with the last letter.

Player 3: "A"—they also realize that Player 4 is stuck with the word "hospital."

Player 4: "L"—they lose.

Player 4 collects the letter "D" for losing a round, the next time they lose it's the letter "R," then "O," then "P," until Player 4 becomes a DropOut and leaves the game.

If you add a letter you have to have an end word in mind. If the other players think that you don't they can challenge you. If you can't come up with an end word, then you receive a letter from DropOut. Alternatively, if someone challenges you about your end word and you have got a legitimate word in mind, then they collect a letter from DropOut.

Suffix This!

A suffix is an ending that is added to a word to form a derivative word. For example, "ment" is added to "commit" to form "commitment."

It can also be added to "state" to form "statement." And when you come to think about it there are lots of "ment" words—arrangement, enlargement, agreement, and so on.

Go round the car in a circle, getting everyone to add a word to the list. There's no need to be editorially picky, it's supposed to be fun, so allow non-suffixes like "moment" or "comment" to keep the game going.

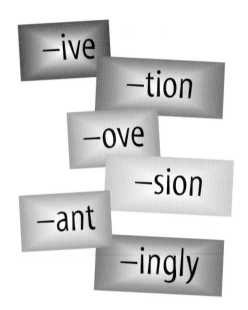

Other endings to words you can try:

-ly	-sion	-ive
-tion	-ant	-ove
-ent	-ingly	

Prefix That!

Instead of putting something at the end of a word, put something at the beginning—this is known as a prefix. For example "pre" can be added to the word "occupy" to form "preoccupy."

It can also be added to "mature" to form "premature" or form words like prepossess, preshrunk, prepaid, premarital, prehistoric, and prejudge.

Other prefixes you can try:

Im-   Mis-

In-   Re-

Un-   Sub-

Dis-   Out-

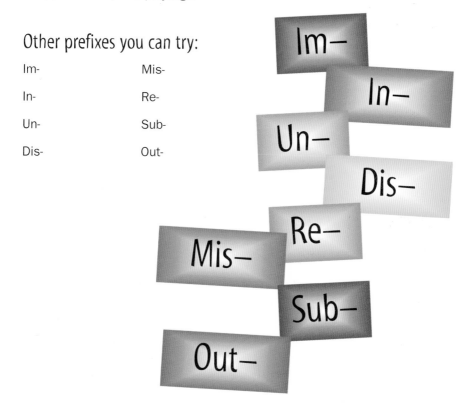

Colors

This is a straightforward game where players have to keep thinking up objects that are associated with a certain color.

Either play as individuals, in sequence, or all together, shouting the objects out.

Things that are **green** such as: grass, leaves, plants, hedges, gooseberries, apples.

Things that are **black** such as: coal, cats, dogs, tarmac, oil, police uniforms.

Things that are **red** such as: fires, autumn leaves, fire engines, strawberries.

A-Zs

Playing A-Zs is a great game for the car and it's an educational one too. Each player takes it in turn to use the next letter of the alphabet to name a certain subject or object.

The great joy of this game is that you can make it as difficult as you want by choosing your subject accordingly.

Cars and car names: Aston Martin, Buick, Chevrolet, Dodge, Eldorado, Ford, Ginetta...

Younger:

Animals: aardvark, beaver, crocodile, dolphin, elephant, frog, giraffe...

Girls' names: Anna, Britney, Chelsea, Diane, Ellie, Fay, Grace...

Boys' names: Ashley, Barnie, Charles, David, Edward, Finton, George...

Older:

Trees: ash, beech, chestnut, Douglas fir, elm, fig, giant redwood...

Countries: America, Botswana, Chile, Denmark, Egypt, France, Ghana, Hungary...

Towns and Cities: Akron, Baltimore, Cleveland, Dallas, El Paso, Fort Lauderdale...

Playing Tips

Set a time limit on answers to get them thinking then bong them out for the last five seconds (which the other kids love doing), Bong, Bong, Bong, Bong, BONG!

Give players three "passes" so you can skip difficult letters.

Fizz Buzz

Fizz Buzz is a game that can be played in the car, in airport departure lounges and it may even go off to college with your kids and get played late night in dorms.

Players decide on a "Buzz Number" between zero and nine (though two can get a bit frantic and nine makes the game very long-winded). Here, we'll make the buzz number three. Players have to count numbers out loud, going round in a circle, but they can't use the buzz number or its multiples.

Play would go like this:

Player 1: One

Player 2: Two

Player 3: Buzz

Player 4: Four

Variation

To get younger children involved in the game, you can limit it to fizz and buzz numbers without the multiples. So using the numbers three and five, there would be buzzes on three, 13 and 23 and fizzes on five, 15 and 25 etc.

Player 1: Five

Player 2: Buzz

To add extra interest a "Fizz" number is thrown in. This has to be a different number—a good one to pick is five. So now the sequence goes:

Player 1: One

Player 2: Two

Player 3: Buzz

Player 4: Four

Player 1: Fizz

Player 2: Buzz

When it gets to numbers that are multiples of both—such as 15 and 30 and 45—players have to shout out "Fizz Buzz!"

If a player gets a number wrong they're out—though it's probably best just to have a point against them, because the more people in the ring, the livelier it is.

Signpost Lottery

There are hundreds of ways of playing signpost games and one of the easiest is Signpost Lottery. Apart from being a fun game it can also sharpen up everyone's mental arithmetic.

For this game you need to look out for roadsigns that give the mileage to various destinations.

If two players are playing, then one chooses to score every top-line mileage and one chooses to score every bottom-line mileage.

As the car passes a roadsign with mileage distances on, it's a battle to see whose mileage is the largest, top or bottom. For example:

Boston	**126**
Cambridge	**84**
Norwich	**105**

Top line mileage player wins by 21 miles, so his/her score moves to 21. Bottom line mileage player scores nothing.

If there is just one destination on the roadsign, then it's no score—because top mileage and bottom mileage are obviously the same!

Variations

Because roadsigns often have different numbers of towns and cities on them (anything from one to six destinations on a sign) the third player option is a complicated one. For this scenario it's a question of suck it and see. If you do have a third player who wants to get involved, they can score all the roadsigns where there is just one destination mileage. They can also score on roadsigns where there are three destination mileages and the middle one is the highest. (For four, five or six: tough luck!)

If your route has roadsigns that start with lowest mileage top and the highest mileage bottom—and many do—then swap around after each sign.

NORWAY	14 M
PARIS	15 M
DENMARK	23 M
NAPLES	23 M
SWEDEN	25 M
POLAND	27 M
MEXICO	37 M
PERU	46 M
CHINA	94 M

Similes and Anti-Similes

You can play around with similes in a number of ways. A simile is an expression that likens one thing to another. For example, cunning as a fox, stubborn as a mule, fit as a flea, mad as a hatter, or hungry like a wolf.

One variety of the game is to play Guess The Simile. For this, a player thinks up a well-known simile and leaves out one of the elements, so the rest of the car has to guess the full expression: As _____ as a board. (*The answer is stiff*).

Or it could be done this way round: As old as the _____. (*The answer is hills*).

Or you could play **Anti-Similes**. For this you have to substitute a rhyming word for the object of a well-known simile. Players take it in turns until they can't think of any more.

Here are some examples of anti-similes: as drunk as a punk, mad as a platter, I slept like a frog, he's as stubborn as a rule, to be strong as a box, cunning as some socks, and helpless as a maybe (baby).

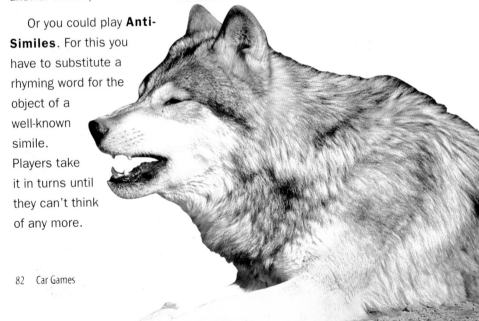

Alliteration

This is more of a comedy game for enjoyment than a game to score points and win. Players have to produce a sentence using words starting with the same letter.

For example: Sally sucked a single sweet stupidly. Or: Timmy's train trundled through the tundra.

It's quite a hard task so you are allowed to use linking words such as "and," "but," "while," "though," "if," "or," and "then" to keep the sentence going, as well as the words "the" and "a," but that's all.

See how long you can keep going before bursting out laughing. Sometimes it's useful to have a pencil and paper to hand just to note down the very worst strangulations of the English language.

General Knowledge

The Business Of Ferrets

There are some amazing collective nouns for animals. The word for a group of ferrets isn't a group, posse, or tribe—it's a "business" of ferrets.

This is a guessing game and you can use the list below over and over till your kids know them all off by heart.

Apes—a shrewdness of apes

Magpies—a tittering, or a tiding of magpies

Elks—a gang of elks

Moose—a gang of moose

Pups—a litter of pups

Owls—a parliament, or a stare of owls

Ferrets—a business of ferrets

Moles—a company, a labor, a movement, or a mumble of moles

Ravens—an unkind-ness of ravens

Rooks—a parliament, a clamor, or a building of rooks

Bears—a sloth of bears

Caterpillars—an army of caterpillars

Woodpeckers—a descent of wood peckers

Racoons—a nursery of racoons

Goldfinches—a charm of goldfinches

Hedgehogs—an array of hedgehogs

Pelicans—a pod, or a scoop of pelicans

Eagles—a convocation of eagles

Peacocks—a muster of peacocks

Vipers—a den, or a nest of vipers

Beavers—a colony of beavers

Rabbits—a warren, bury or nest of rabbits

Spiders—a cluster, or a clutter of spiders

Ibis—a crowd of ibis

Toads—a knab, or a knot of toads

Monkeys—a troop of monkeys

Ducklings—a clutch of ducklings

Sandpipers—a fling of sandpipers

Ducks—a puddling, plump, raft, or flush of ducks

Squirrels—a drey of squirrels

Turtle doves—a pitying of turtle doves

Wrens—a herd of wrens

Tigers—an ambush of tigers

Guillemots—a bazaar of guillemots

Budgerigars—a chatter of budgerigars

Barracuda—a battery of barracuda

Pheasants—a brook, or an ostentation of pheasants

Falcons—a cast of falcons

Crows—a murder of crows

Flamingoes—a flurry, regiment, or skein of flamingoes

Nightingales—a match, puddling, or watch of nightingales

Rhinoceros—a crash of rhinoceros

Thrush—a mutation of thrush

Leopards—a leap of leopards

Variations

After reading these you could even make up your own, such as a giggling of schoolgirls, or a Portakabin of builders, or a bunker of golfers.

The Planets

So how much does everyone know about the planets and the solar system?

The Sun

The sequence of planets closest to the Sun is...Mercury, Venus, Earth, Mars, Jupiter, Saturn, Uranus, Neptune, Pluto.

The Sun is approximately...93 million miles away (150m km).

Size Matters

The biggest planet in the solar system is...Jupiter.

The smallest planet in the solar system is...Pluto.

Pluto is half the size of the next smallest planet, which is...Mercury.

Rings and Moons

Two planets in the solar system have rings...Uranus and Saturn.

Atlas, Pandora, Dione, Helene, and Titan are moons of...Saturn.

Ganymede, Callisto, Europa, Thebe, and Carme are moons of...Jupiter.

Cordelia, Ophelia, Cressida, Portia, and Miranda are moons of...Uranus.

Twinkle Twinkle

The brightest star in the night sky is...Sirius (*Canis Majoris*), the dog star.

Light Fantastic

Light travels from the Sun to the Earth in...8 minutes, 17 seconds.

Reflected light travels from the Moon to the Earth in...1 minute, 26 seconds.

Light travels from the nearest star (*Proxima Centauri*) in our galaxy in...4.22 years.

Light travels from the most distant star in our galaxy in...62,700 years.

Light travels from the edge of the universe in...14 billion years

As Old As The Hills

The Earth is believed to be...4,500 million years old.

The Moon is believed to be...the same age.

The Comet's Tail

The best known comet is Halley's Comet, which returns every...76 years. It's due back in 2062.

Inventions

So how much does everyone know about the world's great inventors? You can ask questions on who invented what and what was invented when...

The hot air balloon was invented by...Jacques and Joseph Montgolfier (France) in 1783.

The ballpoint pen was invented by...John Loud (USA) in 1888.

The bicycle was invented by...Kirkpatrick Macmillan (UK) in 1839.

The car was invented by...Nicolas Cugnot (France) in 1769, though it was used as a tractor to pull guns.

The cash register was invented by...James Ritty (USA) in 1879.

Celluloid was invented by...Alexander Parks (UK) in 1861.

Cinematic film was invented by...Auguste and Louis Lumière (France) in 1895.

The CD was invented by...Philips and Sony (Holland and Japan) in 1978.

The electric lamp was invented by...Thomas Edison (USA) in 1879.

The gramophone was invented by...Thomas Edison (USA) in 1878.

The helicopter was invented by...Etienne Oehmichen (France) in 1924.

The hovercraft was invented by...Sir Christopher Cockerell (UK) in 1952.

The jet engine was invented by...Sir Frank Whittle (UK) in 1937.

The laser was invented by...Dr. Charles H. Townes (USA) in 1960.

The locomotive was invented by....Richard Trevithick (UK) in 1804.

The microphone was invented by... Alexander Graham Bell (USA) in 1876.

The motorcycle was invented by...Gottlieb Daimler (Germany) in 1885.

The neon lamp was invented by...Georges Claude (France) in 1910.

Nylon was invented by...Dr. Wallace H. Carothers (USA) in 1937.

Photography on paper was invented by...W. H. Fox Talbot (UK) in 1835.

Photography on film was invented by ...John Carbutt (USA) in 1888.

The refrigerator was invented by...James Harrison (UK) and Alexander Twining (USA) in 1850.

Rubber tires were invented by... Thomas Hancock (UK) in 1846.

The safety pin was invented by...Walter Hunt (USA) in 1849.

The skyscraper was invented by...William Le Baron Jenny (USA) in 1882, (a dizzying 10 floors).

Stainless steel was invented by...Harry Brearley (UK) in 1913.

The submarine was invented by...David Bushnell (USA) in 1776.

The telegraph code was invented by...Samuel B. Morse (USA) in 1837.

The refractor telescope was invented by...Hans Lippershey (Holland) in 1608.

The television was invented by...John Logie Baird (UK) in 1926.

The thermometer was invented by...Galileo Galilei (Italy) in 1593.

The washing machine (electric) was invented by...Hurley Machine Co. (Chicago, USA) in 1907.

The water closet was invented by Sir John Harington (UK) in 1589.

The zip fastener was invented by Whitcomb L. Judson (USA) in 1891.

Capital Gains

A test of memory here: see how many State capitals and capital cities from around the world your children know. It may even be a refresher for the grown-ups in the car.

You can test individual players or let the children play as a team

States

Alabama (Montgomery)

Alaska (Juneau)

Arizona (Phoenix)

Arkansas (Little Rock)

California (Sacramento)

Colorado (Denver)

Connecticut (Hartford)

Delaware (Dover)

Florida (Tallahassee)

Georgia (Atlanta)

Hawaii (Honolulu)

Idaho (Boise)

Illinois (Springfield)

Iowa (Des Moines)

Kansas (Topeka)

Kentucky (Frankfort)

Louisiana (Baton Rouge)

Maine (Augusta)

Maryland (Annapolis)

Massachusetts (Boston)

Michigan (Lansing)

Minnesota (St. Paul)

Mississippi (Jefferson
City)

Montana (Helena)

Nebraska (Lincoln)

Nevada (Carson City)

New Hampshire
(Concord)

New Jersey (Trenton)

New Mexico (Santa Fe)

New York (Albany)

North Carolina (Raleigh)

North Dakota (Bismarck)

Ohio (Columbus)

Oklahoma (Oklahoma
City)

Oregon (Salem)

Pennsylvania (Harrisburg)

Rhode Island (Providence)

South Carolina (Columbia)

South Dakota (Pierre)

Tennessee (Nashville)

Texas (Austin)

Utah (Salt Lake City)

Vermont (Montpelier)

Virginia (Richmond)

Washington (Olympia)

West Virginia (Charleston)

Wisconsin (Madison)

Wyoming (Cheyenne)

Countries

Afghanistan—Kabul

Algeria—Algiers

Argentina—Buenos Aires

Australia—Canberra

Austria—Vienna

Bangladesh—Dacca

Belgium—Brussels	Italy—Rome	Sudan—Khartoum
Bolivia—La Paz	Jamaica—Kingston	Sweden—Stockholm
Brazil—Brasilia	Japan—Tokyo	Switzerland—Berne
Bulgaria—Sofia	Jordan—Amman	Syria—Damascus
Burma—Rangoon	Kenya—Nairobi	Thailand—Bangkok
Canada—Ottawa	South Korea—Seoul	Turkey—Ankara
Chile—Santiago	Kuwait—Kuwait City	U.K.—London
China—Beijing	Lebanon—Beirut	U.S.A.—Washington DC
Colombia—Bogota	Libya—Tripoli	Venezuela—Caracas
Cuba—Havana	Malaysia—Kuala Lumpur	Vietnam—Hanoi
Denmark—Copenhagen	Mexico—Mexico City	Zaire—Kinshasa
Ecuador—Quito	Morocco—Rabat	Zimbabwe—Harare
Egypt—Cairo	Netherlands—Amsterdam	
Ethiopia—Addis Ababa	New Zealand—Wellington	
Finland—Helsinki	Nigeria—Lagos	
France—Paris	Norway—Oslo	
Germany—Berlin	Pakistan—Islamabad	
Greece—Athens	Peru—Lima	
Guyana—Georgetown	Philippines—Manila	
Hungary—Budapest	Poland—Warsaw	
Iceland—Reykjavik	Portugal—Lisbon	
India—New Delhi	Romania—Bucharest	
Indonesia—Jakarta	Russia—Moscow	
Iran—Tehran	Saudi Arabia—Riyadh	
Iraq—Baghdad	South Africa—Pretoria	
Ireland—Dublin	Spain—Madrid	
Israel—Jerusalem	Sri Lanka—Colombo	

It's a Big, Big, Big World

It's quiz time now. Assembled here is a collection of the planet's vital statistics and a chance for you to see how much your children know about the world they live in.

The biggest ocean is...the Pacific, almost 70m square miles (180m sq km).

The second biggest ocean is...the Atlantic, 41m square miles (106m sq km).

The third biggest ocean is...the Indian, almost 29m square miles (74m sq km).

The Gulf of Mexico is... almost 600,000 square miles (1.5m sq km).

The deepest ocean trench is...the Mariana Trench (West Pacific) 35,840ft (10,924m) —so the oceans are deeper than the Earth's tallest mountain.

The biggest desert is...the Sahara, 3.25m square miles (8.4m sq km).

The second biggest desert is...the Australian Desert, 600,000 square miles (1.5m sq km).

The third biggest desert is...the Arabian Desert, 500,000 square miles (1.3m sq km).

The Mojave Desert is...the world's 15th biggest desert, around 13,500 square miles (35,000 sq km).

The world's tallest mountain is...Mount Everest, which is 29,035 ft high (8,850m).

The world's second tallest mountain is...K2 (Chogori), which is 28,250 ft high (8,610m).

The world's third tallest mountain is...Kangchenjunga in the Himalayas, which is 28,208 ft high (8,597m).

The tallest mountain in North America is...Mt. McKinley in Alaska, which is 20,320 ft high 6,194m) and was first climbed in 1912.

The second tallest mountain in North America is...Mt. Logan in Canada, which is 19,850 ft high (6,050m).

The tallest mountain in South America is...Cerro Aconcagua in Argentina, which is 22,834 ft high (6,960m).

The tallest mountain in Africa is...Mt. Kilimanjaro in Tanzania, which is 19,340 ft high (5,894m).

The tallest mountain in Western Europe is...Mont Blanc in France, which is 15,771 ft high (4,807m).

The world's longest mountain range is...the Cordillera de Los Andes in South America, which is 4,500 miles long (7,200km).

The world's second longest mountain range is...the Rocky Mountain range in the USA, which is 3,000 miles long (4,800km).

The world's third longest mountain range is...the Himalaya-Hindu Kush range, which is 2,400 miles long (3,800km).

The world's tallest volcano is...Ojos del Salado in Argentina/Chile, which is 22,588 ft high (6,885m).

The world's deepest depression is...the Dead Sea in Jordan/Israel, which is 1,296 ft (395m) below sea level.

The world's longest glacier is...the Lambert-Fisher Ice Passage in Antarctica, which is approximately 320 miles long (515km).

The world's deepest cave is...the Reseau du Foillis, in the French Alps, which is 4,773 ft deep (1,455m).

The world's most extensive cave system is...the Mammoth Cave system in Kentucky, which was linked with the Flint Ridge system in 1972 to make a combined length of 213 miles (345km).

The world's longest river is...the Nile, which is 4,145 miles long (6,670km). It flows from Burundi through Tanzania, Uganda, Sudan, and Egypt to the Mediterranean.

The world's second longest river is...the Amazon, which is 4,007 miles long (6,448km). It flows from Peru through Colombia and Brazil to the Atlantic.

The world's third longest river is...the Mississippi, which is 3,710 miles long (5,970km).

The source of the Mississippi is... Beaverhead County, Montana, USA. It encompasses the rivers, Mississippi, Missouri, Jefferson, Beaverhead, and Red Rock. It is the longest river in one country and flows from Montana through North Dakota, South Dakota, Nebraska/Iowa, Missouri/Kansas, Illinois, Kentucky, Tennessee, Arkansas, Mississippi, and Louisiana into the Gulf of Mexico.

The world's tallest waterfall is...the Angel Waterfall on the Carrao river in Venezuela, which drops 3,212 ft (979m).

The tallest waterfall in the USA is...Silver Strand in the Yosemite National Park, California, which drops 1,170 ft (356m).

The world's largest lake is...the Caspian Sea in Iran/Kazahkstan, which covers 143,500 square miles (371,000 sq km).

Index

Acknowledgments

Many of the games in the book have been handed down from generation to generation, no doubt ever since Henry Ford first started turning out large volumes of the Model T and the car became the transport of the masses. Some are derivations of games that started life in the home long before the advent of television, and some, such as Bridge Baseball and Cow Football, have been committed to paper for the first time in this book.

I believe that the game of Stone, Scissors, Paper even started life in another culture. The Japanese play *Janken-pon* with *choki* (scissors), *paa* (paper) and *guu* (stone) to decide who goes first instead of tossing a coin.

So a big thank-you to all the original creators of the games, many of which, like Chinese whispers, have taken on their own form over the years.

Most of all I'd like to thank my children; Theo, Isaac and Hetty for unwittingly testing out all the games over the last ten years. The majority were played long before I had an idea to write this book, but their contribution has been invaluable.